WORKSHOP MODELS FOR FAMILY LIFE EDUCATION

PARENT-CHILD COMMUNICATION

Donald P. Riley
Kathryn Apgar
John Eaton

Family Service Association of America
44 East 23rd Street
New York, New York 10010

Library of Congress Cataloging in Publication Data

Riley, Donald P.
    Parent-child communication.

    (Workshop models for family life education)
    Bibliography: p. 151
    1. Parent and child--Handbooks, manuals, etc. 2. Interpersonal
communications--Handbooks, manuals, etc. I. Apgar, Kathryn, joint
author. II. Eaton, John, 1942-(Mar. 1)-   joint author. III.
Family Service Association of America. IV. Title. V. Series.
HQ755.85.R54   362.8'2   77-13652
ISBN 0-87304-157-7

Final manuscript prepared by Dolores Matarazzo.

Printed in the U.S.A.

PREFACE

<u>Workshop Models for Family Life Education</u> is a series of manuals intended to promote the exploration of new alternatives and the utilization of new options in day-to-day living through programs in family life education.

Basically, family life education is a service of planned intervention that applies the dynamic process of group learning to improving the quality of individual and family living. The manuals are in workshop format and offer possible new approaches of service to families. They are meant to serve as a training mechanism and basic framework for group leaders involved in FLE workshops.

In 1974, the Family Service Association of America appointed a National Task Force on Family Life Education, Development, and Enrichment. One of the goals of the Task Force was to assess the importance and future direction of family life education services within family service agencies. One of the recommendations of their report was to "recognize family life education, development, and enrichment as one of the three major services of the family service agency: family counseling, family life education, and family advocacy."[1] This recommendation was adopted by the Board of Directors of FSAA and has become basic policy of the Association.

---

1. "Overview of Findings of the FSAA Task Force on Family Life Education, Development, and Enrichment" (New York: Family Service Association of America, May 1976), p. 21 (mimeographed).

An interest in family life education is a natural development of FSAA's role in the strengthening of family life and complementary to the more traditional remedial functions of family agencies. FLE programs can add a new dimension to the services provided by family agencies. They can open an agency to the general population by providing programs which are appropriate for all families and individuals, not only for those at risk. They provide a new arena for service that deals with growth as well as dysfunction. They can encourage agencies to look beyond the therapeutic approach and to take on a new objective for the enrichment and strengthening of family life. For the participants, FLE programs can lead to increased understanding of normal stress, growth of esteem for one's self and others, development of communications skills, improved ability to cope with problem situations, development of problem-solving skills, and maximization of family and individual potential.

This series provides tangible evidence of FSAA's continuing interest in family life education and of a belief in its future importance for family services. FLE programs, coordinated within a total agency program and viewed as a vital and integral part of the agency, can become key factors in family service concern for growth and development within all families.

W. Keith Daugherty
General Director
Family Service Association
of America

TABLE OF CONTENTS

INTRODUCTION

The Family Service Association of Greater Boston has a long history
of providing Family Life Education (FLE) services to our client
population. The major thrust of the FLE program has been the parent
discussion workshops. Although we were pleased with the apparent
results of these workshops, we believed that the FLE program could
be enriched by development of a model which not only would provide
the participants with information, but also would help them to put
that information to use by developing skills in effective parent-child
communication and problem solving. Our goal was to provide more
structure to FLE through the use of mini-lectures, role playing, and
exercises and to balance these with time for free discussion. In
developing this model we drew on our past experiences in FLE and
techniques from adult education, learning theory, and communication
theory. The favorable response of participants as well as written
evaluations indicated that we were on the right track.

From our experiential base, we then developed a model--the present
manual--that can be used as a general guideline for conducting parent-
child communication workshops and also be helpful for training and
supervision. The more experienced FLE practitioner may use sections
of this manual selectively, although beginning leaders may wish to
adhere more closely to the original model. We encourage you to be
creative and flexible in using the model and to adapt it to suit your
own teaching style. As you test parts of or the total model, you
obviously will develop different ways of presenting material.
You might also devise different techniques or modifications of
the techniques presented.

Even though this model is for parents of adolescents, it can be easily adapted to groups of parents of preschool and elementary school-age children. Different examples can be developed for the mini-lectures and some of the exercises can be modified in order to suit the different age groups.

The success of an FLE group within an agency depends upon a sound theoretical foundation which is enhanced by creativity and flexibility in helping participants to learn and grow. Your enthusiasm, life experiences, and teaching style also will contribute to the success of your FLE practice. It is the authors' wish that this manual will be helpful to you in leading FLE workshops.

Donald P. Riley
Director of Community and
Professional Education

Kathryn Apgar
John Eaton
Family Life Education Coordinators/
Practitioners

Family Service Association
of Greater Boston
Boston, Massachusetts

GENERAL INFORMATION
ABOUT THE WORKSHOP

In this workshop, it is important to keep in mind that the group members will need considerable support from the leader concerning their own adequacy as parents. When you generalize or universalize the group's experiences about how difficult it is for all parents to cope with developmental changes in their children, they will feel less alone and more hopeful about finding solutions.

LENGTH: The workshop is divided into six sessions and is planned to be given over a six-week period. Each session requires one and one-half to two hours. It may be necessary to adjust the length of the sessions to meet individual and group needs.

MATERIALS: A list of the necessary materials follows the brief outline for each session. All the materials used are relatively inexpensive and easily accessible.

MINI-LECTURES: The manual provides the basic information for each lecture, and the assumption is that the leader will modify it to suit his or her style and group.

An easy and effective way to present the mini-lecture is to talk from an outline on a flipchart or blackboard that is prepared prior to the session. This technique holds the participants' attention and visually highlights the key points in the mini-lecture.

There are some advantages in deferring discussion of the mini-lecture until after the practice exercises are done. By that time, the participants have had the opportunity to experience and try to put into practice the theory presented, and this can result in a more meaningful discussion. There is also the danger that discussion immediately following the mini-lecture will use time that is needed for the exercises. There may, however, be some questions that the leader thinks should be handled after the mini-lecture--for example, questions that relate to procedure and/or group process--but an attempt should be made to keep the responses brief.

HOME EXERCISES: The emphasis here should be on the optional character of these exercises. The leader should go over the exercise and, in explaining it, state that some participants in other groups have found home practice exercises to be useful. Emphasize that these are optional and will <u>not</u> be collected at the next session although there will be an opportunity to discuss them. You <u>do not</u> want to have the participants feel as if they are back in school and under pressure to produce for the teacher.

HANDOUTS: Each session has a section of sample handout materials. A list of additional materials that can be used as handouts and where they can be found is included where approriate. Often, a mini-lecture, flipchart outline, or discussion material also will be used as a handout. To avoid repetition, this material appears only once within the session, and notes in the text indicate where else it should be included.

4

SESSION 1

SESSION 1

BRIEF OUTLINE

OBJECTIVE: To involve the participants in the workshop through introductions and the process of objective setting. To develop an understanding of the importance and the dimensions of effective communication with emphasis on "Behavior is a Statement of Feeling."

I. INTRODUCTION - GET ACQUAINTED

    A. Participants fill out identification cards
    B. Leader introduces self
    C. Introduction of members
    D. Statement and Purpose of Workshop
    F. Overview of Course

II. SETTING OBJECTIVES

    A. Leader Sets Stage
    B. Members List Objectives

III. MINI-LECTURE

    A. "Behavior is a Statement of Feeling"
    B. Discussion

IV. HANDOUTS AND HOME PRACTICE EXERCISES

MATERIALS FOR SESSION 1

Identification cards
Pens or pencils for participants
Flipchart or blackboard; feltmarkers or chalk

Outline of course, pages 21-23
Homework Handout, page 24

Additional materials to have available:

Preparing Instructional Objectives by Robert F. Mager. Belmont,
California: Fearson Publishers, 1972.

"Parents and Teen-agers" #490 and "Parent-Teen-ager Communication"
#438 available from: Public Affairs Pamphlets, 381 Park Avenue
South, New York, New York 10016.

"An Adolescent in Your Home," U.S. Department of Health,
Education, and Welfare, Office of Child Development, Children's
Bureau/D.H.E.W. Publication No. (HD) 75-41. Write to:
Superintendent of Documents, U.S. Government Printing Office,
Washington, D.C. 20402

SESSION 1

I. INTRODUCTION - GET ACQUAINTED

A. Fill Out Identification Cards

Ask participants to fill out identification cards as they arrive. (Have card folded in tent shape, fill out both sides.)

Information to be put on card:
Name, plus any other information you think would be helpful for group. For example, if a parents' group, include names and ages of children, and so forth. If husband and wife are both participants, ask each to fill out a separate card.

Cards can be placed on table in front of them or on floor if table is not used.

B. Leader Introduces Self

This statement should include your name, position, title, perhaps formal education and special training, perhaps years and interest in parent education. Use of first name and personal information, such as your marital status and ages of your children, is up to you.

C. Introduction of Members

Your comments to the group should reflect the kind and composition of the group.
For example, if a parents' group, you might suggest going around the circle, having the participants introduce

themselves, and telling the group the names and ages of their children and where they live.

D. Statement and Purpose of Workshop
    Refer to the need for the workshop as identified by the sponsoring organization and something about your knowledge of the group. In describing the purpose of the workshop, stress positively what they will get out of it; for example, if a parents' of teen-agers group, "You will be more effective in understanding and communicating with your teen-ager and in building a closer relationship. You will be better equipped to solve everyday problems that arise between you and your teen-ager."

    Describe briefly the methodology of the workshop, especially that it will be a nontraditional educational approach, making use of their knowledge and experience and including practice exercises which are the most effective ways to learn and remember new information. Stress that by participating in the exercises, they will be able to transfer this knowledge from the workshop situation to their own homes. Point out that the entire course is designed so that each session builds on the preceding one. Because of this, it is important to stress that the participants try to attend all sessions.

10

E. Overview of Course
    1. <u>Objective</u>: To provide participants an outline of the
        course and objectives and to interest them in the
        course.
    2. Hand out outline of course (see pages 21-23)
    3. Discussion of outline

"I would like to go over briefly what will happen in the
next six sessions. On the outline in front of you, you
will see that in Sessions 2 and 3 we shall be talking about
how we <u>listen</u> and <u>talk</u> to each other. We believe that for
any relationship to be happy and fulfilling, the people
involved must be able to talk and listen to each other
effectively. Thus, before looking at specific techniques
of resolving problems, we shall start with improving your
communication skills. We shall be using the topics and
concerns you have raised as a basis for our discussions.

"In Sessions 4 and 5 we will learn how to use some effective
problem solving skills. These two sessions will include
mini-lectures, practice exercises, and group discussions.

"The major part of the sixth session will be spent on open
discussion. During this session, you will be able to discuss any additional concerns or questions that you have.

"We shall conclude with an evaluation. We feel this is
helpful for you to pull your thoughts together about the
course and also for us so that we can learn from your ideas
about these six weeks.

"This has been a quick look at what we shall cover. There is a great deal of material and a lot to learn. We have also allowed time in each session for an open discussion of your individual concerns and interests. The result will be increased knowledge and skills in talking, listening, and problem solving."

II. SETTING OBJECTIVES

A. Leader Sets Stage

"We will now spend some time working together to decide what each one of you hopes to get out of this workshop. Think about how you would state your interests and concerns in words to the group. After each of you has a chance to do this, we will make a list of each person's interests and concerns. After the session, I will combine similar concerns and bring the list to the next session. We have found this to be the best way to include and work with each person's concerns effectively."

NOTE - <u>Preparing Instructional Objectives</u> is a very practical book explaining how to set learning objectives.

B. Members List Objectives

Choose one of the following methods of eliciting participant's learning objectives:

1. Pair Interviewing

   The leader asks each participant to choose a partner, someone they do not know well, to ask what they hope to learn from the workshop; then they reverse roles. Allow approximately five minutes for this exercise.

   Pair interviewing has been found by experience in groups to be the best way to obtain and then work with each person's concerns, to "break the ice" and form group cohesiveness quickly; this can be explained to the group preceding the task.

At the end of the exercise, the large group is reformed and the interviewers report the partners' learning objectives to the group. The leader lists these on a flipchart or blackboard. An alternative, less time-consuming method of reporting back is to ask one partner to report for both. If there is an odd number of members, the extra person may join one of the pairs.

or,

2. Go-Round

Each person in turn states what he hopes to learn from the workshop.

or,

3. Volunteer

Leader asks participants to volunteer to state their learning objectives as they feel ready or as they wish to share them with the group.

III. MINI-LECTURE

Present mini-lecture in your own words, modifying it to suit
your style and your group. You will want to assess the group's
learning needs, expectations, and past learning experiences
and then adapt this suggested content according to your judgment. New material drawn from personality theory about the
developmental stage of adolescence can be very effectively
used in this model.* A simple and informal way to present
the material is to list key ideas on a flipchart or cards
large enough for people to read. The flipchart also serves
as a guide for your talk. Groups tend to respond more posi-
tively when the mini-lectures include such visual aids.

A. Objective:
   To start participants thinking about the feelings underlying behavior and the need to tune in to those feelings
   as a means of better understanding the behavior.

B. "Behavior is a Statement of Feeling"
   "I want to review and then discuss with you a concept
   which underlies how we see parent-child relationships.

   "Behavior is a statement of feeling. For example, a
   teen-ager provoking his brother is saying, without words,
   something about how he is feeling inside. The teen-ager

---

*See bibliography for suggested readings.

who says 'I like supper' is also stating a feeling. This applies to parents as well. All of our behavior--spanking, hugging, and so forth--is saying how we are feeling. A first step in communication is to try to understand behavior and the feelings behind it. Let me give another example. Suppose your fifteen-year-old son, Jim, comes home in a sour mood. He grumbles when you say hi; he throws his coat down; and he yells at his brother. He is acting nasty and says he is not going out that night. This is strange behavior because he left for school feeling great. He was talking about the good time he and his girl were going to have that night. You assume, probably correctly, that something is wrong between him and his girlfriend. This situation is a more obvious example than often will happen. But the point to understand is that feelings are always behind behavior.

"What might be some of the feelings behind the behavior if something did happen between him and his girl?"

Ask the group to come up with a list. Emphasize the variety of possible feelings.

1. feelings are hurt
2. anger at the girl
3. fear of what his friends will say to him
4. shame
5. feels something is wrong with him - he is weird

"What might be his parent's feelings in a situation like this?"

1. frustrated - what do I say?
2. angry - what's the big deal - he is always upset
3. concerned - how can I talk with him about this? How can I get him to tell me about what happened?

To summarize:

"A basic concept underlying all that we will be discussing is that behind behavior are important feelings. To be able to talk with each other and to solve problems, you must first start by thinking about and identifying what you and your child are feeling."

B. Discussion

1. Can you think of situations where you recognize feelings behind some behavior?
2. Are there any ideas you did not understand or with which you disagree?

IV. HANDOUTS AND HOME PRACTICE EXERCISES

A. <u>Handouts</u>

1. <u>Objective</u>: The objective is to provide the participants with an overview of adolescents and to stimulate their thinking.

2. Pamphlets

"Parents and Teen-agers"

"Parent-Teen-ager Communication"

"An Adolescent In Your Home"

(See page 8 for information on ordering pamphlets.)

3. The pamphlets should be passed out at the end of the meeting. The leader can briefly mention the contents of the pamphlets.

B. <u>Home Practice Exercises</u>

1. <u>Objective</u>: To help the members continue their learning on their own between meetings.

2. The leader should go over the handout (see page 24); in explaining the exercise, state that some participants in other groups have found home practice exercises to be useful. Emphasize that these are optional and will <u>not</u> be collected at the next session although there will be an opportunity to discuss the exercise. The emphasis here should be on the optional. You do not want to have the participants feel as if they are back in school under pressure to produce for the teacher.

HANDOUTS

FOR

SESSION 1

OUTLINE OF COURSE

SESSION 1

OBJECTIVE: To involve the participants in the workshop through
introductions and the process of objective setting.
To develop an understanding of the importance and
the dimensions of effective communication with emphasis
on "Behavior is a Statement of Feeling."

Statement and Purpose of Workshop

Setting Objectives for Workshop

Mini-lecture: "Behavior is a Statement of Feeling."

SESSION 2

OBJECTIVE: To develop skill in listening through mini-lectures,
discussions, and practice exercises.

Discussion of Objectives Selected for Workshop

Mini-lecture: Sensitive Listening and Responding

Practice Exercise on Sensitive Listening and Responding

21

SESSION 3

OBJECTIVE: To develop skill in expressing your thoughts and feelings through mini-lectures, discussions, and practice exercises.

Mini-lecture: Sensitive Expressing

Practice Exercise on Sensitive Expressing

SESSION 4

OBJECTIVE: To develop skill in using the ABC Method of Problem Solving through mini-lectures, discussions, and practice exercises.

Mini-lecture: The ABC Method of Problem Solving

Practice Exercise using The ABC Method of Problem Solving

SESSION 5

OBJECTIVE: To develop further the skill of the participants in using the ABC Method of Problem Solving through the use of practice exercises.

To plan an agenda for Session 6 based on the group's learning needs.

Role Plays Using The ABC Method of Problem Solving

Reassessment of Learning Needs and Initial Objectives

Plan for Session 6

SESSION 6

OBJECTIVE: To encourage the participants to discuss their individual concerns and questions. To enable the participants to apply the skills learned in the workshop as they relate to their specific concerns and questions.

Discussion of Individual Concerns and Questions

Review of Basic Concepts Covered in Workshop

Evaluation of Course

Graduation Certificates Presented

SESSION 1

HOME PRACTICE EXERCISE

How to Understand and Build a Better Relationship

with Your Child

Behavior is a Statement of Feeling

In the first session you learned that you can begin to understand a problem or discover the meaning of your child's behavior by applying the principle, "Behavior is a Statement of Feeling." This principle simply means that feelings are not only expressed by the words you hear, but especially by what your child does. This assignment will help you look for feelings in the actions you observe as well as the words you hear.

Observe a situation between yourself and your child. Describe the situation.

1. Identify and list any feelings your child may be experiencing.

    1.
    2.
    3.
    etc.

2. Identify and list any feelings you are experiencing.

    1.
    2.
    3.
    etc.

24

SESSION 2

SESSION 2

BRIEF OUTLINE

OBJECTIVE: To develop skill in listening through mini-lectures, discussions, and practice exercises.

I. OPENING THE SESSION

    A. Objective
    B. When to Begin
        1. Free Interaction
        2. Procedure for Inclusion of New Participant(s)
    C. Review of Home Practice Exercises

II. OVERVIEW OF SESSION 2

    A. Results of Setting Objectives
        1. Handout: Listing of Objectives
        2. Explanation and Brief Discussion of Workshop's Learning Objectives

III. MINI-LECTURE - SENSITIVE LISTENING AND RESPONDING

    A. Objectives:
       To develop an awareness of how we listen and respond to people.
       To increase skills in listening and responding.
    B. Mini-lecture

IV. LEARNING SENSITIVE LISTENING AND RESPONDING THROUGH PRACTICE EXERCISES

   A. Listening Exercise
   B. Listening and Responding Exercise

V. HANDOUTS AND HOME PRACTICE EXERCISES

   A. Handouts:
      Sensitive Listening and Responding Guide
      Nonverbal Clues
   B. Home Practice Exercise

MATERIALS FOR SESSION 2

Note pads, pencils for all participants
Master list of objectives (see sample pages 51-52)
Handouts (see page 54)
Flipchart or blackboard; feltmarker or chalk
Home practice exercise (see pages 55-57)

SESSION 2

I. OPENING THE SESSION

A. Objective:
The objective for the few minutes before the formal session begins is for the leader to encourage beginning group cohesiveness and relationships through the open interaction between participants and the leader.

B. When to Begin
The leader can expect, in this session and for those to follow, a ten-minute delay for late arrivals. During this period, we suggest some of the following procedures:

1. Free Interaction

   Free interaction can provide useful informal feedback on the first session. It also allows the leader to get a feel for "where participants are" in terms of their interests.

2. Procedure for Inclusion of New Participant(s)

   If new participants arrive for the second meeting, the leader needs to:

   a. Introduce them to the other people
   b. Help them fill out an identification card
   c. Bring them briefly up to date on what happened in the first session, which would include giving them the handouts used.

C. Review of Home Practice Exercises

The ten minutes before beginning the session can also be used to review briefly with the participants their experience with the home practice exercises. This should be done in a casual, informal way to avoid any sense of pressure. The leader can ask if anyone did the exercise and, if so, would they share their experience.

II. OVERVIEW OF SESSION 2

A. Results of Setting Objectives

1. Handout: Listing of Objectives

   From the list of learning objectives stated by the participants in Session 1, you will develop a master list prior to the second session. This is done by looking for similarities and natural groupings of participants' objectives.

   See the example on pages 51-52 of how you might list the group objectives. The specific method of listing the participants' objectives is left to your discretion and creativity. The important aspect of this part of the workshop is that the participants realize their individual concerns have been heard and will be dealt with in the workshop. For any new participants, a suggested procedure is to have them check off the objectives on the sheet that apply to them and to include any additional learning objectives.

2. Explanation and Brief Discussion of Workshop's Learning Objectives

   Explain how the list relates to the content in the session, and, if indicated, ask for group reactions.

III. MINI-LECTURE - SENSITIVE LISTENING AND RESPONDING

An easy and effective way to present the mini-lecture is to talk from an outline on a flipchart or blackboard. This should be prepared prior to the session. (See example on page 53.) You will hold the participant's attention and visually highlight the key points in the mini-lecture.

A. Objectives:
   To develop an awareness of how we listen and respond to people.
   To increase skills in listening and responding.

B. Mini-lecture*
   Distribute copies of Sensitive Listening and Responding Handout (page 54). Material on Handout can also be used on flipchart for easy reference.

   "Today and next week we will be talking about communication and some of the things you can do to improve your talking and listening skills. Communication skills are needed to build better relationships with people. The basic principles can be used in all your relationships. In this

---

*The concepts in this mini-lecture are based on original ideas developed by Janis Ardell in Share Course, an unpublished pamphlet developed at the Family Service Agency of Marin County, San Rafael, California, in 1973, pp. 1-7.

workshop we will be applying the talking and listening skills to improving communication and relationships with children.

"We have two major goals for today's session:
  (1) to help you to notice how you listen and talk to your child; and
  (2) to assist you to develop and increase your listening skills.

"In this workshop we will be defining communication as a process of giving and getting information. Very often we need to <u>get</u> more information to understand what the talker means. A well known example of <u>giving</u> the wrong information is of the parent who gave a sex lecture in answer to her child's question: 'Mommy, where did I come from?' As you may recall, the child wanted to know in what city he was born.

"An important principle I want to highlight is that <u>all communication skills are learned</u>. How to talk and how to listen are skills that we learn beginning in early childhood and continue to learn throughout our lives. We are taught by our families, friends, teachers, and the culture in which we live. As parents, we teach our children rules for communicating we may not even know we have. The pressures of living in today's world exert a hidden but powerful influence over <u>how</u> and <u>when</u> we listen and talk to each other.

"These pressures have conditioned parents and all adults to complete tasks before stopping and listening to a child. In reality there are very few things that we have to get done that are more important than building a relationship with our children. This is a concept that can be applied to couples' relationships as well as to the relationship between parent and child.

"Sometimes we teach openly and directly by telling a child how to talk and act, but we also teach our children by what we do. For example, you tell your teen-ager he may use the family car if he first checks with the other family members, if he will keep it serviced as needed, and perhaps most important, if he drives responsibly. Your teen-ager will also notice if we do those things we ask him to do.

"Today we will look at two things you can do to build a better relationship and to listen more effectively to your child.
1. How to hear your child's feelings.
2. How to let your child know you understand how he feels.

You can probably think of some of the ways teen-agers express feelings. It's easy to understand what he feels when he says it straight out in words.

'I think Mr. Green marked me unfairly after I worked so hard.'

'Thanks for the help Mom, now I can work the rest of the math problems myself.'

The words in these examples are clear and there's no doubt about the meaning and the feeling. But often the feelings are hard to figure out and some exploration is needed if you want to get at the true meaning of what your son or daughter is communicating. Consider these examples.

'I hate school, nothing goes right!'

'That Judy, she's stuck-up!'

'Dad, what's the use of discussing it with you, you'll never understand.'

"What can a parent do in situations like these if you want to build a better relationship? The first step you as the listener can take is to ask yourself the question, 'What feelings am I hearing?' The answer to that question will be found not only in the words, but in the nonverbal parts of the message which includes your child's appearance, expression, tone of voice, behavior such as mannerisms, or actions such as door slamming.

"Here are some common nonverbal clues you can look for in the talker to help you 'hear' feelings."

NOTE: The following material should be put on the flip-chart for easy reference during mini-lecture and used as a handout for participants.

NONVERBAL CLUES TO LOOK FOR IN THE TALKER

Appearance   - does he look alert, dragged out?

Expression   - does he look uptight, worried, angry, cool and calm
                  with little expression, pleasant, friendly?

Tone of voice   - loud, shouting, soft, warm?

Mannerisms   - nervous and jumpy or relaxed and comfortable?

Behavior   - slamming, banging, acts tired, poor appetite, with-
                  draws into room, talks/does not talk with family/
                  friends, dramatic change in interests, activities,
                  play?

ADDITIONAL FACTORS THAT MAY INFLUENCE WHAT THE TALKER MEANS AND FEELS

The different value systems of adults and children.

Expectations   - does he expect people including parents to understand,
                 be helpful; does he see himself as a successful/unsuc-
                 cessful person?

Knowledge   - how much does he know about the issue under discussion?

"If you will look for these nonverbal clues which are present in all communication, you will stand a better chance of understanding more fully what the talker means. Of course, you cannot expect to be aware of all these nonverbal clues, but if you can tune in to one or two of them you will come closer to 'hearing' the talker's feelings and understanding the talker's real meaning.

"This applies to children of all ages; pre-school, latency, and adolescent.

"When you want to hear another person's feelings and want to let them know that you have heard and understand, you can use a method we call Sensitive Listening and Responding. Sensitive Listening and Responding is a tool that will help you to understand the meaning of what the talker says and does. Sensitive Listening and Responding accepts and respects the other person's feelings. When you are listening and responding in this way, you avoid undermining self-esteem by means of cross-examining, blaming, judging, or giving hasty opinions and advice. This method of listening builds self-confidence and independence in the talker and a closer and better relationship between talker and listener. It can lead to the talker taking responsibility for his actions and for solving his own problems."

(Explain the Sensitive Listening and Responding Guide you have handed out prior to beginning the mini-lecture.)

IV. LEARNING SENSITIVE LISTENING AND RESPONDING THROUGH PRACTICE EXERCISES

Following are two exercises on Sensitive Listening and Sensitive Responding. We suggest that you choose only one of the exercises, because it is difficult to use both exercises and still have adequate time for group discussion. It is important to explain the purpose thoroughly and to let the group know that you are building a foundation with the communication exercises for later problem solving. If you have a chart with the steps of the communication-problem-solving model, a brief review of where they are in the process helps to integrate their learning.

A. Exercise One - Listening Exercise
   1. Objective: To increase the participant's awareness of nonverbal communication and of the variety of feelings that underlie all communication.
   2. Suggested procedure
      The following exercise has been found to be useful in helping people integrate the material presented in the mini-lecture.
      a. Reviewing the section of the mini-lecture on non-verbal communication, explain that you wish to discuss with the group the variety of feelings behind non-verbal behavior.
      b. Explain what you mean by using this example:

      "Tim, your fifteen-year-old son, has never been one to watch a lot of television. Since school started three weeks ago, however, he has gone to sit in

front of the television immediately after dinner.
He also seems to be eating more than usual. The
periodic trips to the kitchen from the television
never seem to stop. You mentioned once your concern about his not doing homework and got some
vague reply.

"His feelings might be:

    Frustrated - the work seems too hard at
               school

    Confused   - the teacher's explanation
               about the homework is poor,
               he is confused

    Anxiety   - it's hard to start back to
               school after vacation

    Depressed - he's upset about something,
               for example, his girl breaks
               up with him.

"His parent's feelings might be:

    Anger   - he's not trying

    Frustration - my attempts to help have
               not helped

    Puzzlement - he's always been a good
               student

    Concern   - he won't get into college

    Helplessness - I don't know what to do about
               this situation."

Be sure to emphasize the variety of feelings possible. Point out that you did not get into solutions to the problem. This will come later.

c. Divide the group into two, three, or four subgroups depending on size of group.

d. Have the subgroups appoint a recorder.

e. The task will be to discuss an example of an interaction at home that a member of the subgroup wishes to talk about and to arrive at a list of feelings behind the behavior of both parent and child that will be reported back to the larger group.

f. Allow approximately ten minutes for the subgroups to work. The leader will need to circulate to each subgroup to offer assistance. Subgroups may have difficulty in choosing an example, choosing a recorder, or staying on the subject. Remind them after five minutes that they have five more minutes.

g. Discussion: Ask each subgroup to review briefly their situation and the feelings listed. Put the subgroups' list on a blackboard or flipchart while they are reporting back. Ask the larger group to add their own ideas to the rest of the subgroups. Emphasize the variety of feelings that can lie behind all behavior.

3. Added instructions for leader

a. Thoroughly read over the above instructions so you will be able to explain in your own words your purpose and procedures. It is helpful if the basic instructions for the exercises are on a flipchart or blackboard.

b. Time and number of subgroups: Two hours are
    needed to run this session which would include
    the mini-lecture and one of the exercises. If
    you have less time, choose one of the shorter
    exercises. The number of subgroups depends on
    the leader and the time needed for discussion
    (the more subgroups, the longer this will take).
    For groups of twenty, this takes considerable
    time, often as much as forty-five minutes.

c. The group may shift into talking about solutions
    to the situations given. This should be expected.
    A leader can handle this by:

    (1) Reminding the group of the step-by-step method.
         Recognize that taking the time to consider
         all possible feelings in any piece of nonverbal
         behavior is a time-consuming process but is
         the best way to sharpen their observation
         skills. Point out that if they can become
         more accurate observers of the range of feel-
         ings in any situation, it is more likely that
         they will achieve success in eventual problem
         solving.

    (2) Listen briefly to the suggestions for solutions
         and point out how people naturally feel a need
         to move quickly into "solving" a problem.

    (3) Point out that often people jump to solutions
         before really having listened to all the feel-
         ings and thoughts involved. Ask the group to
         consider whether they fall into that group

when listening. Most groups can accept the
delay in getting the solutions if given
enough explanation and support by the leader.

   d. Discussion of the exercise is vital for integration, sharing of learning, and enhancing group
   cohesiveness. Be sure to allow sufficient time.
   At least thirty minutes at the end of the session
   is needed for discussion following a practice
   exercise.

B. Exercise Two - Listening and Responding Exercise

   1. Objective: To increase participants' awareness of how
   well they listen to what another person is saying to
   them and to develop skills in listening and responding.

   2. Suggested procedure
   The emphasis in this exercise will be on understanding
   not only the words in the statement, but also the
   underlying feelings.

      a. Refer to the mini-lecture on communication-
      sensitive listening; explain that the group will
      break into subgroups for an exercise on how well
      we listen and how we can respond to what we hear.

      b. Ask for a volunteer so you can demonstrate the
      Sensitive Listening exercise. This demonstration
      is suggested because it makes it easier for the
      group to do the exercise if they have seen an
      example.

      c. The volunteer is asked to complete the statement,
      "I love my child but sometimes I..." (the parent

can fill in a feeling such as worry about, concerned about, can't stand) his or her..." (the
parents are to fill in some behavior of the child,
either verbal or nonverbal). Give the volunteer
an example such as: "I love my child but I can't
stand her sloppiness."

d. The leader's task is to try and understand what
the volunteer is thinking and feeling. The leader
will only say "It seems you feel..." or "It seems
you think..." when responding. The leader is to
explain this to the group before proceeding with
the volunteer's example.

e. The volunteer is to explain his statement. The
leader will try to get as clear an understanding
of the volunteer's feelings and thoughts regarding
his statement as possible.

f. After completing the example, divide the group
into pairs. Each pair will have a talker and a
listener. They are to do exactly as the leader
and the volunteer did. Remind them to: say only
"It seems you feel..." or "It seems you think..."
if they are the listener. This is an exercise in
their listening and understanding. Try to get as
much understanding as possible of your partner's
thoughts and feelings.

g. Allow five to ten minutes for this exercise.
After about half the time has elapsed, remind
them they have only so many minutes left.

h. Discussion
   (1) Have the group reassemble and ask each dyad
       to report their experience.
   (2) Highlight in the discussion of their experiences
       the following points:
       (a) Good communication starts with good listening
           - listen to verbal and nonverbal cues.
       (b) What did you learn about yourself as a
           listener?
       (c) Behavior is a statement of feeling. To
           understand what a child or adult is communi-
           cating one must be aware of the meaning of
           the words and the feelings behind them.
       (d) Good communication involves the checking
           out of the meaning of messages sent by the
           communicator to the listener.
       (e) What did you learn about your concern
           regarding your child's behavior?

       (This list is not exhaustive so emphasize your
       own ideas and any that you feel are important
       that came from your group.)

3. Added instructions for the leader
   a. Read over the above instructions thoroughly so that
      you will be able to explain in your own words your
      purpose and procedures. The basic instructions for
      the exercise can be on a flipchart or blackboard.
   b. The group may have difficulty just saying "It seems

you feel" or "It seems you think." We are conditioned
to accept words at face value, rather than to explore,
perhaps because this is sometimes seen as intrusive.
The obvious problem this pattern of listening creates
is that the listener is put in the position of
responding without sufficient information.

V. HANDOUTS AND HOME PRACTICE EXERCISES

A. Handouts
   1. Objective: The objective is to reinforce, through the
      printed material, what the members have learned through
      mini-lectures and class practice exercises.
   2. Suggested Procedure - The handouts on Sensitive Listening
      and nonverbal clues (see example) should be distributed
      prior to the mini-lecture. The leader can briefly mention
      that they contain the main points from the mini-lecture.

B. Home Practice Exercise
   1. Objective: The objective is to help the participants
      continue this learning on their own between meetings.
   2. Suggested Procedure - The leader should go over Session 2
      Home Practice Exercise, and in explaining the exercise,
      state that some participants in other groups have found
      home practice exercises to be useful.

HANDOUTS

FOR

SESSION 2

EXAMPLES OF GROUP LISTINGS
OF
GOALS FOR PARENTS OF ADOLESCENTS WORKSHOP

COMMUNICATION

To learn: (a) how to listen to what our children are saying

(b) how to express what we feel and think to our children

(c) how to encourage our children's listening and talking

(d) how to bring out their good qualities

EVERYDAY QUESTIONS/SITUATIONS

To learn different ways:

(a) to handle fighting between children in the family; to understand the effect teen-agers have on younger children

(b) to help our children study enough

(c) to handle fads

(d) to handle being boy or girl "crazy"

(e) to deal with their not handling their responsibilities, such as not cleaning their room, not doing dishes.

(f) to recognize when our children are taking more responsibility

(g) to deal with their moodiness--crying one minute and happy the next

WHAT TO EXPECT OF CHILDREN

To learn why our children:

        (a) are moody

        (b) want to be so independent

        (c) want a great deal of privacy

FEELINGS ABOUT BEING PARENTS

To learn how to:

        (a) keep calm

        (b) be consistent

        (c) foster dependence appropriately

        (d) decide how permissive or how strict to be

        (e) feel good about the job we are doing as parents

        (f) not be a "buffer" between our children and our spouse

        (g) settle differences in handling situations with our spouse

        (h) deal with our goals and values being different from our children's

        (i) feel comfortable in talking about drugs, alcohol, and sex

IMPROVING COMMUNICATION AND BUILDING RELATIONSHIPS
WITH TEEN-AGERS
BY
"HEARING" FEELINGS AND LETTING THEM KNOW THAT YOU "HEARD"

TODAY'S GOALS

1. To notice how I listen and talk
2. To develop listening skills

Communication is giving and getting information.

All communication skills are learned.

Taught directly/indirectly by families, friends, teachers, culture.

Examples when:

Feelings are clear

Feelings are puzzling

Ask: What feelings am I hearing?

Nonverbal Clues to Look For

Appearance

Facial Expression

Tone of Voice

Mannerisms

Behavior

Other Possible Influences

Values

Expectations

Knowledge

WHEN YOU WANT TO USE SENSITIVE LISTENING AND RESPONDING
TO
"HEAR" YOUR TEEN-AGER'S FEELINGS

SENSITIVE LISTENING AND RESPONDING

Tool to understand feeling and meaning, accepts, respects feelings.

Avoids: cross-examining, blaming, judging, giving opinions, and advice.

BUILDS: Self-confidence, independence, responsibility for solving own problems, better relationships.

1. ### Sensitive Listening

   Listen for hidden messages in words and actions.
   Avoid judgments, criticisms.
   Avoid giving solutions.
   Listen with caring and understanding.

2. ### Sensitive Responding

   Check out your understanding.
   Repeat listening and checking out if necessary.

DON'T USE SENSITIVE LISTENING AND RESPONDING IF:

   it's not needed
   the timing is off
   you feel impatient or can't accept the feelings.

54

SENSITIVE LISTENING AND RESPONDING
TO "HEAR" FEELINGS

I. SENSITIVE LISTENING

Be an accurate observer

Listen for hidden messages (in words and motions)

Avoid undermining self-esteem (comment on the behavior not the person)

Avoid giving hasty solutions (saying ought to, must, should, or else!)

II. SENSITIVE RESPONDING

Check out the accuracy of your observations (regarding the person's feelings and meaning)

Repeat sensitive listening and checking out (until the other person agrees you understand what he feels and means)

Checking out examples: Do you mean...? Are you feeling...? You seem to feel....

DON'T TRY TO USE SENSITIVE LISTENING AND RESPONDING IF

1. The Timing is Off - One or both of you might feel too upset to use it. If this is so, let your child know that you are feeling too upset to talk right now, but that because you think it is important, both of you will talk later.

2. You Don't Have the Time or Energy to Really Listen - Wait until another time and let him know when that might be. There is the danger here of letting "time" itself "handle" the problem. Too often many people feel the best solution is to let time pass instead of becoming involved in listening.

55

The main point to keep in mind is that it is important to respond to every situation even if your response sets a later date to talk together.

3. <u>You are Feeling Impatient, or Can't Accept His Feelings</u> - If you feel "he shouldn't feel that way," work first on understanding what your own feelings are; also remember that feelings do change, yours and your teen-ager's.

<u>NOTE</u> - Sometimes you might want to check out with your spouse or friend whether to use this way of listening.

SESSION 2

HOME PRACTICE EXERCISE

Building a Better Relationship with Your Child
Through Communication Skills
Learning to "Hear" Your Child's Feelings

To communicate with your child and build a closer relationship with him use <u>Sensitive Listening</u> to see and hear the hidden messages in what he says and does; use <u>Sensitive Responding</u> to let him know you understand and to check out with him whether you have "heard" his feelings accurately. <u>Sensitive Listening and Responding</u> accepts your child's feelings, does not focus on judgment, and does not give solutions.

It is much easier to notice how other people listen and respond to us and harder to notice this in ourselves. During the week, try to notice how <u>you</u> listen and respond to others and to your child.

Observe a situation and describe below.

<u>The Situation</u>

<u>How I Listened</u>

<u>How I Responded</u>

ADDITIONAL MATERIALS TO BE USED AS HANDOUTS

Brief Outline for Session 2

"Nonverbal Clues to Look for in the Talker" on page 37.

SESSION 3

SESSION 3

BRIEF OUTLINE

OBJECTIVE: To develop skill in expressing your thoughts and feelings through mini-lectures, discussions, and practice exercises.

I. OPENING THE SESSION

   A. Objective
   B. Review of Home Practice Exercises

II. OVERVIEW OF SESSION 3

III. MINI-LECTURE - SENSITIVE EXPRESSING

   A. Objectives:
      To develop an awareness and basic understanding of how we express ourselves to people.
      To develop and increase our skills in using Sensitive Expressing.
   B. Mini-Lecture

IV. LEARNING SENSITIVE EXPRESSING THROUGH PRACTICE EXERCISES

   A. Exercise One - Styles of Communication
   B. Exercise Two - Sensitive Expressing

V. DISCUSSION AND REVIEW OF MINI-LECTURE AND EXERCISES
GENERAL REVIEW OF SESSIONS 2 AND 3

   A. Review of Principles
   B. Integration of New Learning

VI. HANDOUTS AND HOME PRACTICE EXERCISES

   A. Handout: Guide for Using Sensitive Expressing
   B. Home Practice Exercise

VII. REASSESSMENT OF LEARNING NEEDS AND CURRICULUM
DEVELOPMENT

MATERIALS FOR SESSION 3

    Handouts (see handout section pages 85-88)
    Flipchart or blackboard, feltmarker or chalk
    Note pads, pens or pencils
    Home Practice Exercise (see page 89)
    Flipchart material from Session 2, for review

SESSION 3

I. OPENING THE SESSION

    A.   <u>Objective</u>:
        To continue building group cohesiveness and relationships
        by using the free interaction between the leader and class
        members prior to the formal start of the session.

    B.   During the ten minutes before you formally start the
        meeting, inquire about the home practice exercises and
        discuss them if indicated.

II. OVERVIEW OF SESSION 3

Using the Outline for Session 3, the leader should give a brief overview of what will be happening during this session. Informing the participants of the structure and content of the meeting enhances learning by helping the participants feel more comfortable. Also, by highlighting the key learning events to be covered through sharing the session's plan, you are increasing their interest in the session.

III. MINI-LECTURE - SENSITIVE EXPRESSING

A. <u>Objectives</u>:
   To develop an awareness and basic understanding of how
   we express ourselves to people.
   To develop and increase our skills in using Sensitive
   Expressing.

B. <u>Mini-lecture</u>*
   Distribute copies of handout "Guide for Using Sensitive
   Expressing" (see pages 85-86). It may be helpful to use
   also as a guideline for the mini-lecture on the flipchart.

   "Session 2, we talked about using Sensitive Listening and
   Responding to build a closer relationship with your child.
   Another way to strengthen your relationship is by sharing
   your thoughts and feelings with him. There are many times
   you will want to let your son or daughter know your personal
   ideas, feelings, values, and expectations. When you want
   to 'share' yourself, and at the same time build your relationship, you can use Sensitive Expressing. A good example
   of when to use Sensitive Expressing is in problem solving.
   The skills learned in Sensitive Expressing and Sensitive
   Listening are crucial for effective problem solving.
   Sensitive Expressing follows the same rules as Sensitive
   Listening.

---

*Janice Ardell, Share Course.

66

"Sensitive Expressing suggests commenting on behavior (positive and negative) but not on the person. It also implies that children have the same right to comment on parent's behavior. Through the use of 'I' messages, parents and children can express their positive and negative feelings about behavior as they relate to expectations, plans, agreements, and so forth.

"Let me give you some examples of sharing yourself using Sensitive Expressing:

> 'John, I'm really annoyed that I have to take the time to help you find your school books this morning after I helped you find a convenient spot to put them last night. I'll be late to work. Let's talk about it when I get home tonight.'

"In this example the parent is using 'I' messages to express how she feels about the situation and how she is affected by her son's behavior, leaving no doubt in John's mind how his parent feels, but she does not belittle him as a person and sets the stage for the two of them to discuss the problem further. Here is an example of the same incident in which the parent does not use Sensitive Expressing and where the teen-ager, as a person, is belittled.

> 'John, you are irresponsible! You never do anything right! How many time do I have to remind you to put your school books where you can find them in the morning?'

67

"This parent is using name calling and offers her own solution, which is to put the books where John can find them. John is likely to feel angry, put down, and incompetent as a person. He is so busy feeling badly about himself and resentful toward his parent that it is unlikely he will even think of a solution to the problem. In the first example, parent and child will feel closer as parent shares feelings and shows respect for the teen-ager's feelings (and avoids giving a solution); in the second example, John and his parent will not be creating good feelings between each other and the distance between them will widen.

"Here is another pair of examples:

'Mary-Jo, I'm very pleased that you washed the dishes. It's a relief to me not to have to take the time to do them.'

(After Mary-Jo washed the dishes.) Silence. No recognition given of Mary-Jo's help even though mother felt relieved of the chore.

"In the first example the parent lets Mary-Jo know how good she feels about getting the help; in the second example, she does not express how she feels and says nothing.

"When you want to share yourself, your own thoughts, feelings, and expectations, you can follow the Guide for Using Sensitive Expressing (page 85-86).

"It is not always easy to express our thoughts and feelings openly. At times we try to hide our true feelings. Instead of saying straight out what we really think or feel, we may cover up by taking on the role of a placater, a blamer, a computer, or a distracter.* When we do this, we may be feeling helpless ourselves, but what comes out is blaming someone else; or we are feeling discouraged, disappointed, or sad, but what comes out is anger. It is confusing for the listener because the words say one thing and the face, body, breathing, and muscles are saying something else. Most of the time we are not aware that we are hiding behind these roles and sending such confusing messages. How do we behave and what are the feelings underlying the behavior when we express ourselves in this way?"

Note: The following material is to be used as a handout as well as in the mini-lecture.

---

*These concepts in this mini-lecture are based on original ideas developed by Virginia Satir in Peoplemaking (Palo Alto, Calif.: Science and Behavior Books, 1972), pp. 59-79.

The Placater

What they say - They will agree with what the other person says or wants. They apologize and seek forgiveness; they take the blame.

How they look - They are on one knee; begging and pleading.

How they feel - They feel worthless and unimportant.

The Blamer

What they say - They will act superior and find fault with everything and everyone else. They are very critical.

How they look - They point an accusing finger and look angry.

How they feel - They feel weak and not successful.

The Computer

What they say - They will talk very calmly and without emotion. They are intellectual.

How they look - They have no expression on their face. Their bodies are straight and still.

How they feel - They feel afraid of being criticized.

The Distracter

What they say - They say a great many things, none of which relates to the subject. They change subjects often.

How they look - They try to move in many directions at the same time. They are "all over the place," spinning around.

How they feel - They feel as though they do not have an important contribution to make and that no one will listen to them.

"If you want to avoid communicating in these four confusing ways, you will express yourself in a way that says what you really, honestly think and feel. You will need to be tuned in to your own thoughts and feelings in order to be successful at expressing yourself honestly. When you know where you stand with yourself, you are then ready to express yourself honestly. This means using 'I' messages and following the guidelines for Sensitive Expressing. After you have expressed yourself sensitively, you can use Sensitive Listening and Responding to 'hear' the listener's response to you."

IV. LEARNING SENSITIVE EXPRESSING THROUGH PRACTICE EXERCISES

These practice exercises are designed to develop an awareness of how we express ourselves and to develop and increase our skills in using Sensitive Expressing.

A. Exercise One - Styles of Communication
   1. Objective: The objective of this part of the exercise is for the participants to experience confusing, non-functional ways of communication.
   2. Suggested procedure
      a. Introduction of the Role Play
         (1) Explain to the group that they will be breaking into smaller groups and each group will role play the faulty communication methods using examples from their own home situations. This exercise also teaches us a good deal about the many forms of communication and about the way we ourselves communicate.
         (2) Introduce the role play by referring the participants back to that part of the mini-lecture which describes the four confusing ways of communicating. It is usually helpful to explain to the group that by experiencing faulty communication methods, it is easier to identify the communication methods which are most productive.

b. Choosing the Example

Ask the group to suggest examples of home situations that can be considered for this exercise. It is often helpful to supply them first with an example before eliciting their responses. (An example could be: a family is planning a trip, the parents want to go and the children do not.) As they respond, write three or four of their suggested situations on the flipchart; the group can then select one for the role play exercise.

c. Assignment of Subgroups, Roles and Styles, and Fictitious Names

(1) Have the participants count off in fours to make one subgroup. Continue this process until all subgroups are formed. Depending on attendance, you may need to have one or two groups of five where two people will function as facilitators or one group of three which will require one of the participants to act both as facilitator and recorder.

It is important for the participants to remember their number because they will be assuming the roles and communication styles listed by number on the flipchart. An example of this could be:

Number One - Role: Father; Style: Blamer
Number Two - Role: Mother; Style: Placater
Number Three - Role: Son; Style: Distractor
Number Four - Role: Daughter; Style: Computer

By following this procedure, participants can readily refer to the chart for their role and style and this considerably reduces the amount of explanations and clarification requested of the leader.

Before starting the role play, ask the participants to choose a fictitious name for the role play. This encourages the participants to be freer in role playing because their role may be quite different from their normal way of relating.

d. Role Play.

Hand out the description of each communication style (see page 70).

Before beginning the role play, it is helpful to review the four styles of faulty communication. The leader should join one of the subgroups and demonstrate the different nonverbal positions that characterize each style and briefly demonstrate each style. It is important for the leader to feel comfortable with this demonstration, so we suggest practicing these styles until you are relaxed in demonstrating them.

(1) After your demonstration, ask the participants in each group to take the nonverbal positions and to interact for about a minute.

(2) The subgroups are now ready to assume the full role play. Remind them of the situation they decided to use. This exercise should take about ten minutes. The participants are requested to

assume the positions of the communication style as they discuss the decided-upon situation. Remind them that they are to avoid coming to solutions because the purpose of the exercise is only to see and feel the various communication styles. One of the problems in poor communication is that many people do not say what they are really feeling. This exercise is _not_ meant to work on solutions, but to increase the participant's awareness of how people can and do hide what they are feeling.

(3) Circulate among the subgroups to offer help where needed. Some groups will need help to get into their roles or styles and need help in staying with them. After about five minutes, remind them they have five minutes remaining for the exercise. The time element is not rigid and can be shortened or lengthened according to the groups' need.

e. Discussion

(1) If you are using both sections of the role play, allow approximately fifteen minutes after each section for discussion.

(2) Following are suggested topics for discussion of Exercise One.

How did you feel in these roles?
How did you feel toward the other "members" of your "family"?

75

Did you see yourself in any of the roles?
Which one?
How did this exercise point up for you the
principles in the mini-lecture on Sensitive
Expressing?
Does anyone in the class have examples from
their own lives where they used either Sensitive
Expressing or one of these styles of communicating?

B. Exercise Two - Sensitive Expressing
    1. Objective: The objective of this part of the exercise
       is for the participants to experience honest and sensitive
       expressing.
    2. Suggested Procedure
       a. Introduction of the role play
          (1) Introduce this part of the role play by saying
              that you want them all to experience now the
              use of Sensitive Listening, Responding, and
              Expressing techniques.
          (2) For this exercise the leader can refer the
              group to the Sensitive Listening and Sensitive
              Expressing Guidelines.
       b. Choosing the example to role play
          Use the example the groups have just been discussing
          in the prior exercise on faulty communication styles.
          Or, if you did not use Exercise One, follow the same
          procedure for choosing an example as outlined in
          Exercise One (page 73).

c. Assignment of Subgroups, Roles

Use the same subgroups you used in the previous
exercise but eliminate styles of communication.
In this exercise, use the Guidelines for Sensitive
Listening, Responding, and Expressing. If you did
not use Exercise One, follow the same procedure for
choosing the subgroups and roles as outlined in
Exercise One, page 73. In this section do not use
fictitious names since the emphasis is on the integration of these skills.

d. Role play

(1) Before actually asking the subgroups to role
play, it is helpful for the leader to demonstrate with one of the subgroups some of the
techniques they are to use in role playing the
situation. The other groups are to observe.

(2) Ask all the subgroups to then role play the
agreed-upon situation. This exercise should
take ten minutes. By slowing down the communi-
cation/problem-solving process you are helping
the participants more fully experience the steps
involved in Sensitive Expressing and Sensitive
Listening which leads to more effective problem
solving. As in other exercises, circulate among
the groups and give help where needed. Remind
them when the alloted time is drawing to a close.

e. Discussion

Reassemble the total group and discuss the following
suggested topics:

(1) How did you feel in each role? How did you feel

toward the other "members" of the "family"?

(2) How did you experience the difference in roles between Exercise One and Exercise Two?

(3) Did you see yourself in any of the roles? Which one?

(4) How did it feel to use Sensitive Expressing?

(5) Do any of the class have examples from their own lives where they have used Sensitive Expressing?

V. DISCUSSION AND REVIEW OF MINI-LECTURE AND EXERCISES AND GENERAL REVIEW OF SESSIONS 2 AND 3

A. Review of Principles

Because this is the last session on communication, it is important to review the principles from Sessions 2 and 3. Without interfering with the flow of the discussion, refer to the Brief Outline for Sessions 2 and 3. These should be put on the flipchart or blackboard.

B. Integration of New Learning

This session may be more gratifying for the participants as they move beyond seeing themselves primarily in a listening role which was the focus in Session 2, to seeing themselves expressing their own thoughts and feelings which is stressed in Session 3. Now that the content on communication has been presented, how to talk as well as how to listen, the participants should now have integrated much of the material from Sessions 2 and 3.

VI. HANDOUTS AND HOME PRACTICE EXERCISES

A. Handout
   1. Objective: To solidify the learning of participants by providing them with visual material covering the key points of Sensitive Expressing.
   2. Suggested Procedure - Distribute the handouts prior to the mini-lecture so that they can follow along with what you are saying.

B. Home Practice Exercise
   1. Objective: To help the participants continue their learning on their own between sessions.
   2. Suggested Procedure - Answer any questions regarding the home practice exercise. It is often helpful to give participants an example of the kind of situation they would use in the home practice exercises.

VII. REASSESSMENT OF LEARNING NEEDS AND CURRICULUM DEVELOPMENT

Hand out the Assessment and Curriculum Planning Sheet (see handout section, pages 87-88). Ask the group members to fill out the sheet during the week because it will be discussed at the end of the fourth session. For the members who do not bring the sheets to the fourth session, have extra copies available that can be filled out at that session.

The leader should mention to the group that it would be most helpful to him/her if they would answer as frankly and fully as possible the questions on the Reassessment of Learning Needs and Curriculum Development Sheet. The group should be told that their comments and suggestions will be helpful to the leader in planning how to meet their identified learning needs.

HANDOUTS

FOR

SESSION 3

Building a Better Relationship with Your Child

Through Communication Skills

Guide for Using Sensitive Expressing

WHEN YOU WANT TO "SHARE YOURSELF" - YOUR THOUGHTS, FEELINGS, VALUES,
EXPECTATIONS
1. "Tune in" to your own thoughts and feelings (self-talk).
2. Use "I" messages. (Express honestly what you feel and think.)
    Hint - Sending "I" messages goes roughly like this:
            "I" feel (describe feeling) when (describe situation)
            because (describe what you need or how you are affec-
            ted).
3. Avoid expressing hasty conclusions while trying to use
    Sensitive Expressing.
4. Avoid using judgments (such as name calling, criticism)
    that undermine your child's self-esteem.
5. Check out your understanding of your child's feelings.
    (Use Sensitive Listening and Responding here.)
6. Repeat Steps 1, 2, 3, 4, if needed.

DON'T USE SENSITIVE EXPRESSING IF
    You or your child do not have the time, energy, patience, or
    desire to use it - set a date for another time.

ADVANTAGES OF USING THIS METHOD
1. Builds relationship.
2. Children feel trusted and respected.
3. Many problems will be solved if parents and children allow themselves time to use Sensitive Listening and Expressing.
4. Parent feels he/she has truly expressed self. Feels good.

Reassessment of Learning Needs

and Curriculum Development

SINCE BEGINNING THIS WORKSHOP:

How frequently do you use Sensitive Listening in everyday situations?

Seldom_____

Sometimes_____

Often_____

How frequently do you use Sensitive Expressing in everyday situations?

Seldom_____

Sometimes_____

Often_____

WITH WHOM DO YOU USE:

Sensitive Listening?

Spouse_____

Children_____

Friends_____

People at Work_____

Sensitive Expressing?

Spouse_____

Children_____

Friends_____

People at Work_____

87

Please check off how helpful the following methods have been for you in your learning thus far.

	Most Helpful	Somewhat Helpful	Least Helpful
Handouts			
Home Practice Exercises			
Mini-Lectures			
Discussion			
Practice Exercises - Role Play			

What parts of Sensitive Listening were most difficult for you?

What parts of Sensitive Expressing were most difficult for you?

Any additional comments?

SESSION 3

HOME PRACTICE EXERCISE

Building a Better Relationship with Your Child

Through Communication Skills

Sharing Yourself with Sensitive Expressing

Describe a situation in the past week in which you used "sharing your-self" (Sensitive Expressing) communication with your child to help build a closer relationship.

SITUATION

HOW DID YOU SHARE YOURSELF? - SENSITIVE EXPRESSING

HOW COULD YOU HAVE IMPROVED THIS COMMUNICATION?

EXAMPLE

Ineffective   "Mary Ellen, you are inconsiderate and lazy when you don't vacuum the floor like you promised."

Sharing Yourself   "Mary Ellen, I feel very disappointed when I see the vacuuming still needs to be done and I don't have time to finish the job before my guests arrive."

ADDITIONAL HANDOUT MATERIALS:

The Brief Outline for Session 3

The descriptive 'cover' roles on page 70.

SESSION 4

SESSION 4

BRIEF OUTLINE

OBJECTIVE: To develop skill in using the ABC Method of Problem
Solving through mini-lectures, discussions, and practice exercises.

I. OPENING THE SESSION

   A. Free Discussion
   B. Review of Home Practice Exercise

II. OVERVIEW OF SESSION 4

III. MINI-LECTURE - THE ABC METHOD OF PROBLEM SOLVING

   A. Objective
   B. General Instructions
   C. Mini-Lecture

IV. LEARNING THE ABC METHOD OF PROBLEM SOLVING THROUGH
    PRACTICE EXERCISES

   A. Objective:
      To enable participants to develop and increase their skills
      in using the ABC Method of Problem Solving through use
      of practice exercises.
   B. Problem-Solving Exercise.

V. HANDOUTS AND HOME PRACTICE EXERCISES

    A. Handouts: The ABC Method of Problem Solving
    B. Home Practice Exercise on Problem Solving

VI. REVIEW OF REASSESSMENT OF LEARNING NEEDS AND
CURRICULUM DEVELOPMENT

94

MATERIALS FOR SESSION 4

Flipcharts or blackboard, feltmarker or chalk
Note pads, pens or pencils
Handouts (pages 111-113)
Home practice exercise (pages 114-115)

SESSION 4

I. OPENING THE SESSION

A. <u>Free Discussion</u>
The leader should anticipate that by this session the
participants will be volunteering their questions and
concerns about previous sessions. Through this discussion,
the leader should then be able to assess the degree of
integration of material previously presented and from that
assessment determine which material should be reviewed
with the group.

B. <u>Review of Home Practice Exercise</u>
During the ten minutes you wait to start the meeting,
inquire about the home practice exercise and discuss
if indicated.

II. OVERVIEW OF SESSION 4

Using the Brief Outline, the leader can briefly review
what will be happening during this session. By informing
the participants of the structure and content of the meeting,
the key learning events to be covered can be anticipated.

III. MINI-LECTURE - THE ABC METHOD OF PROBLEM SOLVING

A. Objective:

For participants to learn the steps of The ABC Method of Problem Solving.

B. General Instructions

The problem-solving method presented in this session integrates the listening and expressing skills into a problem-solving format. This results in an approach that is highly useful and therefore of great interest to the participants. It is, however, a more complex method to learn than the listening and expressing methods, partly because the listening and expressing skills, just being integrated into learning, are also used throughout the problem-solving process. For this reason, more time will be needed for learning.

It will probably be most helpful if the learning is divided into two stages. The first learning stage takes place in this session and focuses on assisting the participants to familiarize themselves with what goes into each step of the problem-solving method. The mini-lecture starts this learning by providing the ABC model for the participants. There is a suggested flipchart outline in this session (see page 111). Actual problem situations supplied by the participants can be used to practice each step of the problem-solving process utilizing small sub-group discussion techniques.

The second stage of learning builds on the participants
growing familiarity and comfort with the concepts.

By the fifth session the participants are ready to use
the problem-solving concepts in a role play or a problem
situation. The entire fifth session can be devoted to
several role plays to reinforce learning. It will give
everyone a chance to hear from, and react to, the subgroups' experiences.

D. Mini-lecture*
    This mini-lecture can be used as a handout in conjunction
    with your lecture and is helpful for use in the Home
    Exercise. Copies can be distributed prior to beginning
    this part of the session.

    "Prior to explaining the steps in the ABC Method of
    Problem Solving, I want to mention some initial planning
    and thinking the parent should do. As in Sensitive
    Listening and Expressing, it is vital that the parent and
    child feel that they have the time, interest, and the
    emotional energy to apply the problem-solving process.

---

*Some of the concepts in this mini-lecture are based on original
 ideas developed by Richard Abidin in Parenting Skills: Trainer's
 Manual (Charlottesville, Va.: University of Virginia, Jefferson
 Printing, 1975), pp. 127-33.

"It is also important that both parent and child agree
to try the new methods. The parents must first sensitively
express to the child their desire to try a new way of
solving the problem and encourage them to try this with
them. Your child may very well be nervous about trying
it, as you may be, but if the parent genuinely wants to
try it, most children will agree. If they continue to
resist, through your Sensitive Listening and Responding
skills, you may be able to 'hear' their concerns and
relieve them.

"If a parent finds that they are unable to get started at
all, there may be a need for relationship building. There
are times when the relationship between two people needs
to be improved to a point where the ABC Method of Problem
Solving can take place. Professional couseling can often
be of help in these instances."

Hand out copies of ABC Method of Problem Solving (page 111).

Step A, Defining the Problem Situation
"Your task in Step A is to define, in specific terms, the
factual information about the situation as it applies to
the parent and to the child. This means to look at what
the behavior is that is upsetting to you and your child.
You are not defining vague or global problems such as
your child not being good. You are defining in specific
terms a specific situation. From the parent's view, the
situation may be your child not coming home on time; from
the child's view, the situation may be a school activity

not ending on time. In this step your skills in
Sensitive Expressing, Listening, and Responding are
used.

Step B, Self-Talk

"Your task in Step B is to think about and feel for what
the problem means for you and the child. Give yourself
some time to think about what you and your child are
thinking and feeling.

"In self-talk, ask yourself these questions:

1. What am I feeling? You will be better able to control
    your reactions and responses if you let yourself think
    about what you are feeling.
2. What might my child be feeling? After having some
    time to think about what you are feeling, think about
    your child. Just why is he acting that way? Remember
    that feelings are behind behavior.
3. Has this situation happened before? If it has, how
    did I handle it and did that work? If not, why might
    this be happening now?
4. Am I 'self-talking' thoughtfully or emotionally?
    a. Thoughtful self-talk means that you do ask your-
        self what you are feeling and what your child is
        feeling. You let yourself calm down. You act
        like the parent you are--in charge of the situation.
    b. Thoughtful self-talk means that you do not think
        of who's to blame or at fault. Playing judge only
        makes someone feel like a criminal.

c. Thoughtful self-talk has appropriate expectations. You expect behavior that is appropriate for the age of your child, in contrast to behavioral expectations that you might like but which are unrealistic to expect.

d. Thoughtful self-talk means not over-reacting to your own feelings, and looking at your child's feelings.

e. Thoughtful self-talk means having the courage to face an issue at the time it happens, not to avoid it. Emotional self-talk involves self-talk based on strong emotions. We all have strong feelings. Strong feelings are not bad, but if we base our reactions only on these strong feelings self-talk, the solutions do not work. Intense emotional feelings can interfere with the process of Sensitive Listening and Expressing. These feelings can also interfere in the process of effective problem solving. You will need to take time to examine the reasons for these strong feelings. For example, which feelings are related to the problem situation right now and which feelings are related to past difficulties with the same problem? Is some of what you are feeling not even related to the situation? By taking some time to think about your strong feelings you should feel calmer and better able to proceed with finding workable solutions.

Step C, Reactions and Solutions

"You have 4 tasks in Step C. These are:

1. Search for areas of agreement and disagreement.
2. Brainstorm possible solutions.
3. Choose a solution. It is important to remember not to choose a solution that you cannot carry out, and not to choose a solution that undermines your child's good feeling about himself.

    a. Agreement - The people agree on the solution.

    b. Compromise - Both people involved must give up having their solution used completely; part of each solution is used.

    c. Going Along - One of the persons involved agrees to go along with the other person's solution. This is often done for a period of time as a trial and then discussed further.

    d. Protective - When all attempts at problem solving have failed behavior could result in:

       (1) physical harm to himself or others

       (2) damage to property

       (3) breaking the law.

    The parents have to set firm limits and their solution is used. Some children will respond easily to this approach. When this does not happen, parents may wish to seek professional counseling.

    e. Ignoring - For situations where there is a reasonable degree of certainty that other factors, such as peer pressure or changing fads, will alter the behavior and that parental intervention will not be needed.

4. Put solution into practice. Evaluate how the solution works. It is very important that you plan a time to evaluate the solution at the time you choose it. Build an evaluation into the solution plan.

There may be times when you find the method not working. If you find this happening, you might ask yourself the following questions:

a. Have I and my child _really_ agreed to try this new approach?

b. Is the timing off? Does one of us still feel too angry or upset to really use this method? Is there too much else going on for problem solving to work?

c. Do we need to do more work on the Sensitive Listening and Expressing in Steps A and C?

d. What kind of self-talk did we do? Too much emphasis or emotional self-talk will lead to hasty, emotional, unworkable reactions and solutions. Emphasis on thoughtful self-talk will lead to more thought-out and workable reactions and solutions."

IV. LEARNING THE ABC METHOD OF PROBLEM SOLVING THROUGH
PRACTICE EXERCISES

A. Objective:

To enable participants to develop and increase their skills
in using the ABC Method of Problem Solving through the use
of practice exercises.

B. Problem-Solving Exercise

1. Suggested procedure

Briefly explain that the participants will be forming
subgroups and each subgroup will practice applying the
problem-solving steps to a problem situation they have
brought from their own experience.

2. Introduction of practice exercise

Refer to the problem-solving steps shown on the flipchart
and presented in the mini-lecture and briefly review how
the group should work with each step.

3. Choosing the examples

Ask the total group to suggest examples of home situations
that can be considered for the exercise. It can be helpful to offer an example such as: "My son often does not
tell me he'll be home late from school." Write the
problem situations on the flipchart. If there are fewer
situations than the number of subgroups planned, several
or all subgroups could work with the same situation.

4. Assignment of subgroups

Divide the group into subgroups of three, four, or five
depending on the size of the total group. Each subgroup
is to select a situation from the flipchart they wish to
role play.

5. Problem-solving task group

Each group should be given a worksheet (see handout
section, page 112-113) that shows the problem-solving
steps according to the ABC Method. The group task is to
apply the ABC Method to the problem situation selected.
Ask each group to choose a recorder whose task will be
to record the groups' work at each step of the problem-
solving process. The recorder also shares his ideas
for each step. When the practice exercise is completed,
the recorder reports back to the entire group on the
work his subgroup did on understanding and resolving
the problem situation. Let the group know they will
have fifteen minutes in which to work.

Circulate among the subgroups offering help as needed.
You may observe a pattern of difficulties or successes
the groups are experiencing which you can comment on
during the discussion. The subgroups should complete
all steps. Even though they may feel they are not ready
to move on, it is important to identify what parts of
the problem solving gave the participants the most
difficulty.

6. Discussion

Allow approximately thirty minutes for reporting back
by the recorders from all of the subgroups. If time
permits, a general discussion of the content of the mini-
lecture is also helpful. You might record on the flipchart each subgroup's experience with each problem-
solving step; that is, whether they worked with ease or
difficulty, trying to pinpoint the reasons for the
difficulties, and pooling the entire group's experience.

V. HANDOUTS AND HOME PRACTICE EXERCISES

A. Handouts
   1. Objective: To help solidify participants' learning by
      providing them with visual material covering the key
      points of the ABC Method of Problem Solving.
   2. Suggested Procedure: Give out the handouts prior to
      the mini-lecture so that the participants can follow
      what you are saying.

B. Optional Home Practice Exercise on Problem Solving
   1. Objective: To help the members continue their learning
      on their own between meetings.
   2. Suggested Procedure: By this session the group will feel
      familiar with the home practice exercises. After handing
      them out you can give them an example of the kind of
      situation they would use in the home practice exercise.

VI. REVIEW OF REASSESSMENT OF LEARNING NEEDS AND CURRICULUM DEVELOPMENT

In the last session, the participants were given a handout on Reassessment of Learning Needs and Curriculum Development that they were to fill out prior to this session. Allow ten minutes for open discussion by the participants about the comments, suggestions, concerns, and assessments that they put on the handout. Remind the participants that the sixth session is an open one and that more attention can then be directed toward the areas they are discussing. If possible, make a listing of their stated learning needs. Even though this discussion will be short, it will help you to assess how much learning integration has taken place. It will also help you in the review that will be needed in Sessions 5 and 6 and set the stage for the open discussion in Session 6.

HANDOUTS

FOR

SESSION 4

THE ABC METHOD OF PROBLEM SOLVING

STEP A - Defining the problem situation for parent; for child

STEP B - Self-Talk (thinking and feeling about the problem)
           Emotional
           Thoughtful

STEP C - Reactions and Solutions
           Search for Areas of Agreement
           Brainstorm Possible Solutions
           Pick a Workable Solution
                   Agreement
                   Compromise
                   Going Along
                   Protective
                   Ignoring
           Put the Solution into Practice
           Evaluate how the Solution Works

111

A. STATEMENT OF PROBLEM

                              FACTS

    FOR PARENT   FOR CHILD

B. SELF-TALK - THINKING AND FEELING

                            THINKING

    FOR PARENT   FOR CHILD

                            FEELING

    FOR PARENT   FOR CHILD

112

C. REACTIONS AND SOLUTIONS

1. Areas of Agreement, Disagreement

    Agree   Disagree

2. Possible Solutions

    Agreement, Compromise, Going Along, Protective, Ignore

SESSION 4

HOME PRACTICE EXERCISE

Building a Better Relationship with Your Child

Through the ABC Method of Problem Solving

You have now learned the basic steps in the ABC Method of Problem Solving. If you want to try using this approach during the coming week, use this outline as a guide.

A. <u>Statement of Problem</u>

<u>Facts</u>

<u>For Parent</u>   <u>For Child</u>

B. <u>Self-Talk - Thinking and Feeling</u>

<u>Thinking</u>

<u>For Parent</u>   <u>For Child</u>

<u>Feeling</u>

<u>For Parent</u>   <u>For Child</u>

114

Possible Solutions

Best Possible Solution

ADDITIONAL HANDOUT MATERIALS:

The Brief Outline for Session 4

The mini-lecture beginning on page 99,   The ABC Method of
Problem Solving.

SESSION 5

SESSION 5

BRIEF OUTLINE

OBJECTIVE: To develop further the skill of the participants in using the ABC Method of Problem Solving through the use of practice exercises.

To plan a tentative agenda for Session 6 based on the group's learning needs.

I. OPENING THE SESSION

Review of Home Practice Exercises

II. OVERVIEW OF SESSION 5

III. LEARNING PROBLEM SOLVING THROUGH PRACTICE EXERCISES ROLE PLAY

A. Objective:

To develop further the skill of the participants in using the ABC Method of Problem Solving through the use of practice exercises.

B. Demonstration Role Play

C. Group Role Play

IV. PLANNING FOR SESSION 6

A. Introduction

B. Reassessment of Learning Needs

C. Curriculum Development

D. Preparation for Termination

MATERIALS FOR SESSION 5

Flipchart or blackboard, feltmarker or chalk
Note pads, pens or pencils
Handouts (page 135)

SESSION 5

I. OPENING THE SESSION

Review of Home Practice Exercises

The fourth session hopefully saw the start of the group's
integrating the communication/problem-solving concepts.
Whether the group made use of the home practice exercises
or not, it is very important for the leader to ask for any
feedback from the home practice exercises or from their
attempts to use the ABC Method. Lead a brief discussion
on their initial problems and successes. You will receive
both positive and negative feedback. This is characteristic
of a group beginning to integrate new material. The group
needs to hear often that this is a new technique that takes
time to get used to. If you feel this discussion is starting
to take too much time, ask the group to delay questions and
comments until after the practice exercises, when they can be
discussed further.

II. OVERVIEW OF SESSION

Using the Brief Outline as a guide, explain to the group the plan for this session.

III. LEARNING PROBLEM SOLVING THROUGH PRACTICE EXERCISES -
      ROLE PLAY

   A. Objective:
       For the participants to develop skill in the use of the
       ABC Method of Problem Solving, first, by means of observa-
       tion of a role play and second, by active participation in
       a role play of a problem situation.

   B. Demonstration Role Play
       In this exercise the group members can learn how to use
       the ABC Method by observing the leader and two volunteers
       apply the problem-solving steps to an actual situation.
       The demonstration role play serves two functions--it
       promotes skill learning in use of problem-solving
       techniques and, as a warm-up exercise, reduces anxiety
       about role playing later on their own.
       1. Suggested procedure
           a. Introduction to the Role Play
               Explain to the group that they will be breaking
               into smaller groups for the purpose of role
               playing the actual application of the ABC
               problem-solving steps to a real problem situation
               from their own experience.

               Explain that you will ask two group members to
               volunteer to demonstrate with you a sample role
               play. The group will observe how you and the
               two volunteers apply the ABC Method to a problem
               situation. Refer back to the ABC steps on the

flipchart (see Session 4, page 111), briefly reviewing how the group will be working with each step in the role play.

b. Choosing the Example

Ask the group to suggest examples of home problem situations that can be considered for the role play. It can be helpful to offer an example, such as, "My son often does not tell me he'll be home late from school." Write the suggestions on the flipchart and ask the group to choose one they would like to see demonstrated. Elicit a sufficient number of problem situations to use later when the entire group divides into role-play subgroups.

c. Selection of Volunteers

Ask for two volunteers to join you to demonstrate to the group how to apply the ABC Method steps. If there is some hesitation, emphasize that they do not have to feel that they fully understand how to use the method, that you will be acting as a facilitator to help them with each step, and that this will be an opportunity for the volunteer to get some additional practice. You might ask, "who is or would like to be interested in working on the ...problem?"

d. Role play

Ask the volunteers to decide which role they wish to play (the parent or child) and to select names to use. If the person who volunteered the situation to be role played also volunteers to do the

role, it is often helpful to have that person
role play the child rather than the parent. Begin
Step A by having the players state the problem, as
each of them see it, in a factual and a specific way,
from the parent's viewpoint and from the child's
viewpoint. Spend sufficient time on the statement
of the problem so that each understands how the
other sees the problem. Then move on to Step B,
where they will focus on how each thinks and feels
about the problem. Step B involves tuning in to
themselves. The leader should assist the volunteers
in this process of identifying their thoughts and
foolings about the problem.

The leader might list on the flipchart some self-
talk ideas and feelings. After each volunteer has
completed his self-talk, they are ready to go on to
Step C. The role players now use Sensitive Expressing
to express to each other how they think and feel and
use Sensitive Listening and Responding to let the
talker know they understand.

From this open expression by each one, areas of
agreement and disagreement can be identified by
the volunteers and listed on the flipchart by the
leader. The leader's role involves assisting the
role players to use the Sensitive Listening and
Sensitive Expressing skills while they are progressing
through the problem-solving steps. Possible solutions
can then be offered by the role players; the leader
can assist in the selection of workable solutions

agreeable to both parties.

e. Discussion of Role Play

Begin by asking the players how they felt in the
role and toward their partner. What parts of the
role play or problem-solving process gave them most
difficulty, what was easiest?

Ask the group to comment on what they saw happening,
which parts of the problem solving seemed most
difficult for the role players. Would they have
handled the situation any differently if they had
been in the role play? Can they offer other possible
solutions both might accept? Ask the group if they
have any further questions before they begin the role
play.

C. Group Role Play

1. Suggested Procedure

a. Introduction to the Role Play

The group will be breaking into subgroups of four
for the purpose of role playing the ABC problem-
solving steps with a real problem situation from
their own experience. Explain that they will be
proceeding with the role play in the same manner
as the role play they just observed. There will
also be a recorder who will take notes as the role
play progresses through the problem-solving steps.

b. Choosing the example

If you need additional examples of problem situations
from home, ask the group for them at this time. If

126

there are fewer situations offered than number of subgroups planned, several or all subgroups could work with the same situation.

c. Assignment of subgroups and roles

Divide the group into subgroups of four. (Depending on attendance, you may need to have one or two groups of five where two people will function as facilitators or one group of three which will require one of the participants to act both as facilitator and recorder.)

Each subgroup then will select one of the situations from the flipchart they wish to role play. One of the participants should choose to play the role of parent and one the role of child, and they must select names to use. If the person who volunteered the situation to be role played also volunteers to do the role play, it is usually helpful to have them play the child rather than the parent. The two other participants are to decide which is to be the facilitator and which one will be the recorder.

d. Practice exercise - group role play

As in Session 4, hand out to the recorders the worksheet that shows the problem-solving steps according to the ABC Method (see page 135). Explain that the recorder's task is to record the subgroups' work at each step and, after the role play exercise is completed, to report back to the entire group what happened with the problem solving.

Explain that the facilitator's task is to assist the role players to use the ABC Problem-Solving Method as in the demonstration role play. When the role players reach Step C, the facilitator and recorder join in and share their ideas for possible solutions and assist in the selection of workable solutions agreeable to both parties.

Tell the subgroups that they will have fifteen minutes in which to work.

Circulate among the subgroups offering help as needed. You may observe a pattern of difficulties or successes the groups are experiencing. You can comment on these during discussion. After about ten minutes, remind the groups they have five minutes remaining to complete the exercise. The subgroups should complete all steps. Although they may feel they are not ready to move on, it is important to identify what parts of the problem solving gave the participants the most difficulty.

e. Discussion of Role Play

Begin by asking the players how they felt in their roles and toward their partners. Then ask for feedback by the recorders, possibly listing on the flipchart successes and difficulties experienced by each of the subgroups at each of the ABC steps of problem solving. After all subgroups have reported, raise some of the following questions for discussion:

Can you identify any common experiences shared by all or by a few?

Did you learn anything about how you usually problem solve?

How comfortable did you feel using this problem-solving method?

Did it feel uncomfortable? Did it feel artificial?

How easy or difficult was it for you to use Sensitive Listening and Sensitive Expressing at the same time as you were trying to apply the ABC Method of Problem Solving?

Did this seem like too much to keep in mind?

Was the facilitator of any help; if so, in what ways?

How ready do you feel to try to use this problem-solving method with your own family?

Do you feel this role-playing exercise was useful in helping you to learn how to apply the principles of Sensitive Listening, Sensitive Expressing and problem solving?

If not, can you suggest another way we could work at learning how to problem solve?

IV. PLANNING FOR SESSION 6

A. Introduction

One of the goals of the sixth session is to support the
participants in the continued use of the concepts they
have learned. To do this most effectively, you and the
group need to be clear on what concepts they seem to
understand and what concepts are still confusing. Therefore,
this section of Session 5 is for the group to finish their
reassessments of their learning needs in order to develop
the curriculum for Session 6.

B. Reassessment of Learning Needs

Make use of the Reassessment of Learning Needs sheet filled
out by the group after the third session. The leader will
review these before this session and assess where individuals
are and where the group is in their learning. It may be of
help if you review the following for yourself and the group:

1. What they seem clear on
2. Where they seem confused
3. What added information, practice, or discussion
   topics might be helpful.

C. Curriculum development

The sixth session is primarily planned to meet the open
discussion needs of the participants. Despite the emphasis
on open discussion, you do want to use what you have learned
from the discussion of their learning needs to do some
tentative agenda building for Session 6.

130

Typical agenda items may include:

1. Review of concepts
2. Role play of Sensitive Listening, Sensitive Expressing, Problem Solving
3. Discussion of specific questions or concerns
4. Discussion of developmental material.

The content is up to you and the group. Be certain to include time in the session for evaluation and the awarding of the graduation certificates.

D. <u>Preparation for Termination</u>

You and the group have been planning for termination. This should be mentioned to the group. In order to make it easier for the group to terminate, allow time for the expression of feelings about saying good-by, but do not belabor the point either in this session or in the sixth session. The emphasis should be on the participants' gains and support of their continued use of what they have learned.

HANDOUTS

FOR

SESSION 5

THE ABC METHOD OF PROBLEM-SOLVING WORKSHEET

A. STATEMENT OF PROBLEM

FACTS

FOR PARENT   FOR CHILD

B. SELF-TALK - THINKING AND FEELING

THINKING

FOR PARENT   FOR CHILD

FEELING

FOR PARENT   FOR CHILD

C. REACTIONS AND SOLUTIONS

1. Areas of Agreement, Disagreement

Agree   Disagree

2. Possible Solutions

Agreement, Compromise, Going Along, Protective, Ignore

135

ADDITIONAL HANDOUT MATERIAL

Copies of the Brief Outline of Session 5

Helpful to have on hand copies of the ABC Method of
Problem Solving found in Session 4 on page 111.

SESSION G

SESSION 6

BRIEF OUTLINE

OBJECTIVE: To encourage the participants to discuss their individual concerns and questions.
To enable the participants to apply the skills learned in the workshop as they relate to their specific concerns and questions.

I. OPENING THE SESSION

Presentation of Agenda

II. CONTENT OF SESSION 6

    A. Review of Basic Concepts
    B. Discussion

III. EVALUATION QUESTIONNAIRE

IV. GRADUATION CERTIFICATES

MATERIALS FOR SESSION 6

Flipchart or blackborard, feltmarkers or chalk
Evaluation forms, pencils
Graduation certificates

SESSION 6

I. OPENING THE SESSION

Presentation of Agenda

You will most likely want to have developed a tentative agenda for this meeting. Have this on a flipchart and review this with the group. Stress that this agenda is tentative and the final session is planned to meet the open discussion needs of the participants.

II. CONTENT OF SESSION 6

As indicated above, the discussion will depend upon the content as agreed upon by the leader and the participants. Because of this, the leader will have to make maximum use of his or her group skills. A few suggested guidelines to remember are:

A. Review of Basic Concepts
   If you plan a review of the basic concepts, which is often helpful, use the flipchart guidelines and make the review succinct.

B. Discussion
   A large part of this meeting should be free discussion. This can be fun, rewarding, and a good learning experience for the leader and the group. The emphasis should be on supporting their continued use of what they have learned.

   Every group develops their own list of humorous and frustrating examples of parental attempts to cope with their children. The sharing of these examples gives an opportunity for the leader and the participants to support and encourage continued efforts at problem solving.

   The parent with a specific question can use this time to bring it up. Be sure to encourage this and to involve the group in using the skills they have learned in the workshop as they apply themselves to the specific questions.

III. FVALUATION

Suggested Procedure
Allow approximately twenty minutes for evaluation.

When asking the group to fill out the evaluation form (page 147), mention that they do not need to put their names on them and that these are helpful in planning future courses and in evaluating this one.

After filling out the evaluation form, the group will want to sum up for themselves what they have learned, their experience in the group, and their feelings at ending. You should share openly with the group what you have learned and your feelings about the group.

IV. GRADUATION CERTIFICATES

We believe the awarding of certificates is important for a
number of reasons. A certificate provides a visible reward
and recognition for the participant. We believe it is also
helpful in maintaining the motivation of the group member in
continuing the use of the communication/problem-solving skills
learned.

144

HANDOUTS

FOR

SESSION 6

EVALUATION QUESTIONNAIRE

1. What in the workshop did you find to be most helpful in improving your relationship with your child?

2. Check off how helpful to your learning were the following methods used in the workshop.

	Most Helpful	Somewhat Helpful	Least Helpful
Handouts			
Home Practice Exercises			
Mini-Lectures			
Discussion			
Practice Exercises - Role Play			

3. What questions or concerns do you have that were not covered by the workshop?

4. What suggestions do you have to improve this workshop for other parents?

BIBLIOGRAPHY

BIBLIOGRAPHY

THEORY

Bruner, Jerome S. Toward a Theory of Instruction. New York: W.W.
    Norton, 1968.

Frey, Louise A.; Shatz, Eunice; and Katz, Edna-Ann. "Continuing
    Education - Teaching Staff to Teach." Social Casework, 55:360-68
    (June 1974).

Knowles, Malcolm. "Andragogy: An Emerging Technology for Adult
    Learning." In The Modern Practice of Adult Education. New York:
    Association Press, 1970.

Lidz, Theodore. The Person, His Development Throughout the Life
    Cycle. New York: Basic Books, 1968.

Ortof, Selma D. "The Family Agency as Community Educational Activist."
    Social Casework, 51:28-34 (January 1970).

Pasework, Richard A., and Albers, Dale A. "Crisis Intervention:
    Theory in Search of a Program." Social Work, 17:70-77 (May 1972).

Reynolds, Bertha. Learning and Teaching in the Profession of Social
    Work. New York: Rinehart and Co., 1942. Reprint, New York:
    National Association of Social Workers, 1976.

GROUP PROCESS

Frey, Louise A. " Support and the Group: A Generic Treatment Form."
    Social Work, 7:35-40 (October 1962).

Garland, James; Jones, Hubert; and Kolodny, Ralph. "A Model for Stages
    of Development in Social Work Groups." In Explorations in Group
    Work, ed. Saul B. Bernstein. Kennebunkport, Maine: Milford House,
    1973.

Knowles, Malcolm and Knowles, Hulda. <u>Introduction to Group Dynamics</u>. New York: Association Press, 1959.

MacLennan, Beryce and Felsenfeld, Naomi. <u>Group Counseling and Psychotherapy With Adolescents</u>. New York: Columbia University Press, 1968.

Mann, James. "Some Theoretic Concepts of the Group Process." <u>International Journal of Group Psychotherapy</u>, 5:236-41 (July 1955).

Rose, Sheldon A. <u>Treating Children in Groups</u>. San Francisco: Jossey-Bass, 1972.

Rosenbaum, M. and Berger, M. <u>Group Psychotherapy and Group Function</u>. New York: Basic Books, 1963.

Scheidlinger, Saul. "The Concepts of Social Group Work and of Group Psychotherapy." <u>Social Casework</u>, 34:292-97 (July 1953).

Yalom, Irving. <u>Theory and Practice of Group Psychotherapy</u>. New York: Basic Books, 1970.

TECHNIQUES

Abidin, Richard R. <u>Parenting Skills: Trainer's Manual</u>. Charlottesville, Virginia: University of Virginia, Jefferson Printing, 1975.

Ardell, Janice. "Share Course." Family Service Agency of Marin County, San Rafael, California, 1973.

Auerbach, Ailine B. <u>Parents Learn through Discussion</u>. New York: John Wiley & Sons, 1967.

Galper, Jeffry, "Nonverbal Communication Exercises in Groups." <u>Social Work</u>, 15:71-78 (April 1970).

Gordon, Thomas. <u>Parent Effectiveness Training</u>. New York: Peter H. Wyden, Inc., 1971.

Johnson, David W. <u>Reaching Out - Interpersonal Effectiveness and Self-Actualization</u>. Englewood Cliffs, N.J.: Prentice Hall, 1972.

Knowles, Malcolm. "Designing and Managing Learning Activities."
In The Modern Practice of Adult Education. New York: Association
Press, 1970.

Mager, Robert. Preparing Instructional Objectives. Belmont,
California: Fearon Publishers, 1962.

Otto, Herbert A. "Marriage and Family Enrichment Programs in North
America: Report and Analysis." The Family Coordinator, 24:137-42
(April 1975).

Pfeiffer, J.W. and Jones, John. A Handbook of Structured Experiences
for Human Relations Training. Vol. I, II, III, IV. San Diego:
University Associates, 1974.

Satir, Virginia. Peoplemaking. Palo Alto: Science and Behavior
Books, 1972.

Simon, Sidney B.; Howe, Leland W.; and Kirschenbaum, Howard. Values
Clarification: A Handbook of Practical Strategies for Teachers and
Students. New York: Hart, 1972.

FOR PARENTS AND PROFESSIONALS

Blos, Peter, On Adolescence. New York: The Free Press, 1962.

Group for the Advancement of Psychiatry. Normal Adolescence.
New York: Charles Scribner's & Sons, 1968.

Jones, Molly Mason. Guiding Your Child from 2-5. New York: Harcourt,
Brace, and World, Inc., 1967.

Josselyn, Irene M. The Adolescent and His World. New York: Family
Service Association of America, 1962.

Kiell, Norman. The Adolescent through Fiction. New York: International
Universities Press, 1964.

_____. The Universal Experience of Adolescence. New York: International
Universities Press, 1964.

Senn, Milton J.E., and Solnit, Albert J. Problems in Child Development.
Philadelphia: Lea and Febiger, 1968.

Valentine, C.W. The Normal Child. New York: Pelican Books, 1956.

Winnicott, D.W. The Child, the Family, and the Outside World.
   Baltimore: Penguin Books, 1964.

154